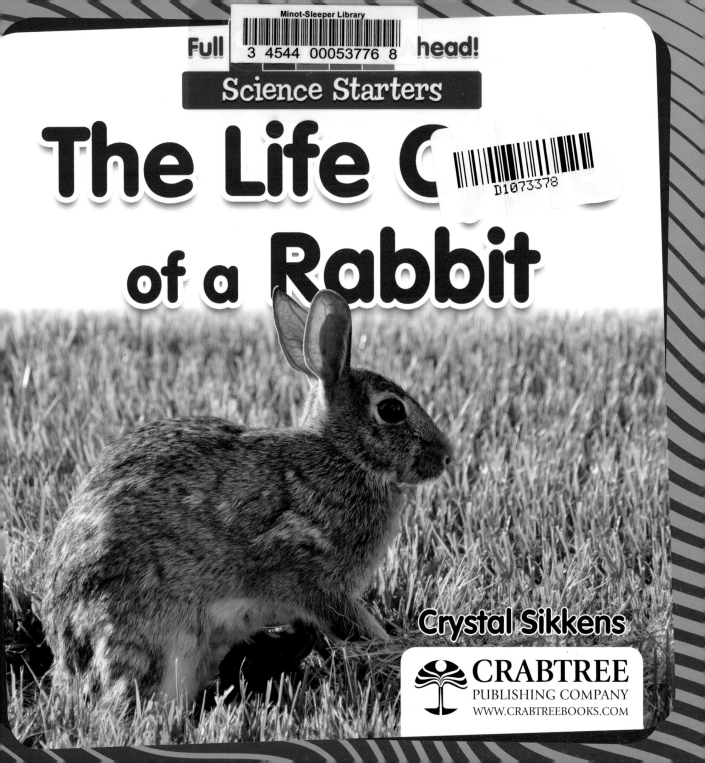

Full **Steam** Ahead!

Science Starters

The Life Cycle of a Rabbit

Crystal Sikkens

CRABTREE
PUBLISHING COMPANY
WWW.CRABTREEBOOKS.COM

Title-Specific Learning Objectives:

Readers will:

- Explain that a life cycle is a series of changes that happens to a living thing in its lifetime.
- Describe the life cycle of a rabbit using learned vocabulary.
- Use images and captions to identify key ideas and features at each stage of a rabbit's life cycle.

High-frequency words (grade one) a, are, at, by, can, have, is, it, of, the, when	Academic vocabulary buck, doe, female, kits, litter, male

Before, During, and After Reading Prompts:

Activate Prior Knowledge and Make Predictions:

Have children read the title and look at the cover and title-page images. Engage children by asking them to show a thumbs-up if they agree or a thumbs-down if they disagree with the following statements:

- Every living thing has a life cycle.
- The rabbits on the front cover are adults.
- The rabbit on the title page is an adult.

During Reading:

After reading page 14, ask children to stop and re-read the caption below the image. Ask:

- What is the main idea of the caption?

- How does the caption help you understand the picture?
  Encourage children to think about how the comparison (the size of baseballs) helps them understand how much the babies have grown.
- Encourage children to pay attention to the captions as tools to help their comprehension.

After Reading:

Talk about how a doe prepares for her babies, then takes care of them after they are born. Make a step-by-step sequence using the words "first, next, and last." Create the same sequence describing the milestones in a kit's growth.

To my amazing daughter Hailey Joy Sikkens, with all my love

Author: Crystal Sikkens
Series Development: Reagan Miller
Editor: Janine Deschenes
Proofreader: Melissa Boyce
STEAM Notes for Educators: Janine Deschenes
Guided Reading Leveling: Publishing Solutions Group
Cover, Interior Design, and Prepress: Samara Parent
Photo research: Crystal Sikkens
Production coordinator: Katherine Berti

Photographs:
Animals Animals: Wild & Natural: p. 16
Dreamstime: Mark Turner: title page, p. 9; Alla Orlova: p. 11
iStock: NickBiemans: front cover; scolson: p. 5; Joseph Kostansek: p. 6-7; XiFotos: p. 10; shanelinkcom: p. 13; stanley45: p. 14
Science Source: Bill Coster/FLPA: p. 8; G. Ronald Austing: p. 12
Wikimedia commons: Jhansonxi: p. 4
All other photographs by Shutterstock

Library and Archives Canada Cataloguing in Publication

Sikkens, Crystal, author
The life cycle of a rabbit / Crystal Sikkens.

(Full STEAM ahead!)
Includes index.
Issued in print and electronic formats.
ISBN 978-0-7787-6200-3 (hardcover).--
ISBN 978-0-7787-6237-9 (softcover).--ISBN 978-1-4271-2256-8 (HTML)

1. Rabbits--Life cycles--Juvenile literature. 2. Rabbits--Growth--Juvenile literature. I. Title.

QL737.L32S53 2019   j599.32   C2018-906157-X
                                               C2018-906158-8

Library of Congress Cataloging-in-Publication Data

Names: Sikkens, Crystal, author.
Title: The life cycle of a rabbit / Crystal Sikkens.
Description: New York : Crabtree Publishing Company, [2019] | Series: Full STEAM ahead! | Includes index.
Identifiers: LCCN 2018056583 (print) | LCCN 2018058648 (ebook) | ISBN 9781427122568 (Electronic) | ISBN 9780778762003 (hardcover : alk. paper) | ISBN 9780778762379 (paperback : alk. paper)
Subjects: LCSH: Rabbits--Life cycles--Juvenile literature.
Classification: LCC QL737.L32 (ebook) | LCC QL737.L32 S534 2019 (print) | DDC 599.32--dc23
LC record available at https://lccn.loc.gov/2018056583

Printed in the U.S.A./042019/CG20190215

Table of Contents

Crabtree Publishing Company

www.crabtreebooks.com   1-800-387-7650

Copyright © **2019 CRABTREE PUBLISHING COMPANY**. All rights reserved. No part of this publication may be reproduced, stored in a retrieval system or be transmitted in any form or by any means, electronic, mechanical, photocopying, recording, or otherwise, without the prior written permission of Crabtree Publishing Company. In Canada: We acknowledge the financial support of the Government of Canada through the Book Publishing Industry Development Program (BPIDP) for our publishing activities.

Published in Canada
Crabtree Publishing
616 Welland Ave.
St. Catharines, Ontario
L2M 5V6

Published in the United States
Crabtree Publishing
PMB 59051
350 Fifth Avenue, 59th Floor
New York, New York 10118

Published in the United Kingdom
Crabtree Publishing
Maritime House
Basin Road North, Hove
BN41 1WR

Published in Australia
Crabtree Publishing
Unit 3 – 5 Currumbin Court
Capalaba
QLD 4157

New Life

When a baby rabbit is born, it begins its **life cycle**. A life cycle is the changes that happen to an animal during its life.

Baby rabbits are called kits or kittens.

A female rabbit is called a doe. A male rabbit is called a buck.

doe

A doe takes care of the kits.

kit

5

Baby Rabbits

A group of kits born at the same time is called a **litter**.

There can be two to twelve kits in one litter.

A doe can have three to five litters each year. Most kits are born between February and September.

Safe Homes

First, a doe builds a place to have her kits. She may build a **nest** above the ground or dig a **tunnel** under the ground.

A tunnel helps keep the kits safe after they are born.

A nest needs to be soft and warm for the kits. A doe uses grass, leaves, straw, and fur for her nest.

This doe collects grass and straw from a field to build her nest.

Newborn Kits

Newborn kits look different from **adult** rabbits. Kits are born with very little fur. They can't see or hear.

Newborn kits stay close together to keep warm.

When the mother rabbit leaves the nest, she covers it with grass and small sticks. This helps hide the nest from other animals.

Eating and Growing

The mother rabbit comes back to the nest each night to feed her babies. Mother rabbits feed their kits milk from their bodies.

Kits only feed for a few minutes once or twice a day.

The kits start to grow fur when they are about one week old. They start to see and hear after about ten days.

Leaving the Nest

By the time the kits are two to three weeks old, they have a full coat of fur.

Three-week-old kits are about the size of baseballs.

By three weeks, the kits are able to hop.
They begin leaving the nest for short times.
They might start **nibbling** on food.

Finding Food

Kits leave the nest to look for food. They start eating plants, such as grass and flowers.

Rabbits eat many different kinds of plants.
They eat fruits and vegetables too!

Kits have to be careful when leaving the nest. Many animals eat rabbits. Kits are small. They are easier for these animals to catch.

raccoon

Foxes, coyotes, and raccoons eat rabbits.

On Their Own

By five weeks old, most kits are ready to live on their own. They no longer drink milk from their mothers.

Rabbits can start a family of their own when they are three to six months old. By one year, most rabbits are done growing. They are now adult rabbits.

Repeating Cycle

All rabbits follow the same life cycle.

Newborn kits

One-week-old kits

The life cycle repeats each time an adult has a new baby. To repeat is to begin again.

Three-week-old kits

Adult rabbit

Words to Know

adult [AD-uhlt] adjective
Fully grown

life cycle [lahyf SAHY-kuhl] noun The changes that happen to an animal during its life

litter [LIT-er] noun A group of babies born at the same time to one mother

nest [nest] noun A safe place built or chosen by an animal to lay eggs or have babies

nibbling [NIB-ling] verb Eating by taking small bites

tunnel [TUHN-l] noun An underground hole

A noun is a person, place, or thing.

A verb is an action word that tells you what someone or something does.

An adjective is a word that tells you what something is like.

Index

About the Author

Crystal Sikkens has been writing, editing, and providing photo research for Crabtree Publishing since 2001. She has helped produce hundreds of titles in various subjects. She most recently wrote two books for the popular Be An Engineer series.

To explore and learn more, enter the code at the Crabtree Plus website below.

www.crabtreeplus.com/fullsteamahead

Your code is:
fsa20

23

STEAM Notes for Educators

Full STEAM Ahead is a literacy series that helps readers build vocabulary, fluency, and comprehension while learning about big ideas in STEAM subjects. *The Life Cycle of a Rabbit* uses sequential text, informational images, and explanatory captions to help readers identify the main parts of a rabbit's life cycle. The STEAM activity below helps readers extend the ideas in the book to build their skills in arts and science.

Displaying a Life Cycle

Children will be able to:
- Draw an image and write a caption to describe each stage of a rabbit's life cycle.
- Create a mobile to display their work.

Materials
- Life Cycle Mobile Planning Sheet
- Life Cycle Mobile Good Copy
- Materials for mobile, including clothes hangers or wire and straws, string, hole punch, card stock, glue, crayons, etc.

Guiding Prompts
After reading *The Life Cycle of a Rabbit*, ask:
- What is a life cycle?
- What are the stages of a rabbit's life cycle?
- How does a rabbit's life cycle repeat?

Activity Prompts
Explain to children that they will create mobiles to hang in the classroom. The mobiles will have cards, placed in order, that show a rabbit's life cycle. Each card has a picture and caption.
- Just like the pictures and captions in the book, each picture and caption on the mobile should clearly explain that stage.

Each child gets a Life Cycle Mobile Planning Sheet. Review the stages of the rabbit's life cycle with children. Create a class anchor chart with the stages, for children's reference.

1. First, a doe builds a nest.
2. Then, a kit is born in a litter. Newborn kits cannot see or hear. They have very little fur.
3. After they are one week old, kits start to grow fur, and they begin to see and hear.
4. By the time they are three weeks old, kits have a full coat of fur and they begin to hop.
5. When they are five weeks old, they stop drinking milk, and leave the nest for food.
6. Finally, rabbits are adults at one year old.

Check children's planning sheets, then give them the Life Cycle Mobile Good Copy. They will cut out the squares and glue them to pieces of card stock. Then, they can build their mobiles.

Extensions
- Make mobiles to display other types of steps.
- Invite children to think about and try other ways of displaying steps, such as creating a flip-book, a slide show, a performance, etc.

To view and download the worksheets, visit **www.crabtreebooks.com/resources/printables** or **www.crabtreeplus.com/fullsteamahead** and enter the code **fsa20**.